# *What You Won't Expect When You're Expecting Because This is The CRAP They Don't Tell You: ABC's of a SUCKY Pregnancy*

I0190568

1

## Also by **T.R. Ipleac**

*Act Like a CEO, Think Like a Millionaire: Why You Should Care LESS about What a Man or Woman Thinks About Love, Intimacy, and Commitment and MORE about GETTING WHAT YOU WANT OUT OF LIFE*

# What You Won't Expect When You're Expecting Because This is The CRAP They Don't Tell You: ABC's of a SUCKY Pregnancy

By T.R. Ipleac

Copyright © 2012 T.R. Ipleac

All rights reserved. Published in the United States and Internationally by TTP Publishing.

No part of this book may be reproduced or transmitted in any form or by any means without written permission from the author.

ISBN: 978-0-9855988-9-1.

# What You Won't Expect When You're Expecting Because This is The CRAP They Don't Tell You: ABC's of a SUCKY Pregnancy

By T.R. Ipleac

**Preface**

**Introduction**

**A – ADVANCED sense of smell**

**B – BREASTS sagging**

**C – CONSTIPATION**

**D – DIARRHEA**

**E – EMOTIONAL**

**F – FLINSTONE feet**

**G – GAS**

**H – HUNGER**

**I – INDIGESTION**

**J – JINX**

**K – KICKING**

**L – LEAKS**

**M – METALLIC taste**

**N – NAUSEA**

**O – OILY skin**

**P – PEEING**

**Q - QUESTIONS about everything**

**R – ROUND ligament pain**

**S – S-T-R-E-T-C-H marks**

**T – TIREDNESS**

**U – UGLY Betty**

**V – VEINS**

**W – WEIGHT**

**X – XTRA hair everywhere**

**Y - YELLOW teeth**

**Z – ZOOM**

**About TTP Publishing**

**TTP Publishing Books**

# Preface

So here is what we do know. You and your hubby, partner, significant other…have a good night. All goes well, and at least one of you orgasms. While you sleep, or eat, or whatever your after-lovemaking session involves, your body goes to work. If you are ovulating, your body has released some eggs, and your hubby's little swimmers are en route to those eggs. If they meet and implant, the result is pregnancy. And that is where it gets interesting.

If you are pregnant, thinking about starting a family, or know someone who is, then you have probably already come across a ton of pregnancy books. Those pregnancy books give the "happy" side of pregnancy and joyfully gloss over or minimize some really serious pregnancy predicaments. On the covers of those pregnancy books, you might see smiling pregnant women, little endearing shots of baby feet, or a beautiful blemish-free pregnant belly. Inside of those "happy" pregnancy books are cute little quips and quotes, sunny and cheerful descriptions of pregnancy symptoms, and an overall positive look on pregnancy. This book is different. Way different.

As a matter of fact, if you are looking for a glossed-over, Hollywood-produced, Tinseltown, PG or G-rated version of pregnancy, then PUT THIS BOOK BACK ON THE SHELF or back into your file folder AND WALK AWAY. That way, you can keep your idealistic view of pregnancy. Stop reading now, and hold on to your dreams of a un-blemished pregnant belly, your belief that nausea is only mildly annoying and reserved for mornings, or that you'll only experience a little bit of tiredness, and the always comical belief that your body will bounce back soon after Junior pops out.

However, if you want a realistic description of the not-so-pretty side of pregnancy; an explanation that will be blatant and maybe even humorous, but is meant to honestly express some real-life experiences of pregnancy and beyond, then stay tuned. This book is for those who are interested in seeing the total picture of what pregnancy can be - and indeed is - for many women. This book is for the pregnant woman with a sense of humor, because with pregnancy, believe me, you're going to need one!

All jokes aside, because there will be plenty more of them to come, this book says what others are afraid to say about pregnancy. This is necessary for a few reasons. One, because no one should go into anything as serious as bringing another life into the world without knowing as much as they possibly can about what to expect. Two, if some women knew what all they should or could expect from pregnancy, they could make more informed decisions, for example, possibly deciding NOT to have children in the first place. I believe that some women might elect not to have children if they knew all of what's involved in such a lifetime-commitment, energy and

11

reserves-draining, thankless endeavor. I also believe that we would judge those women who choose not to have children less harshly.

Whether a woman decides NOT to have children because she doesn't want to ruin her figure, or because she doesn't want to be tied down, or because the sun sets in the West, all of those reasons are legitimate and should be respected. And hopefully by the end of this book they will certainly be understood. Deciding NOT to have children for whatever reason or for no reason at all does not make a woman selfish, it actually makes her responsible because she is making this decision before she brings a child into the world, and before she can do the child any harm.

How many women do we know personally or have heard about that have made us think that maybe they shouldn't have had children? Well, whatever you decide, the decision will be yours to make and you will be able to make it intelligently because you will be well informed. And entertained.

You see, as much as this book is meant to provide information, my sincere hope is that it will make you gasp, laugh, and nod your head in equal parts. Or, at least laugh more often than not. Such is the case with motherhood. One of the great things about motherhood in general, is that it lightens you up and makes you see the world through friendlier eyes. Children have a way of bringing out the inner-child in you. So sit back, and if you're pregnant pull out your pickles and ice cream, and enjoy. Happy reading, happy pregnancy, or if you choose not to have children, be happy that your Saturdays are your own!

--T.R.

# Introduction

WTF was that?!

Have you ever worried about air getting trapped in your vagina and killing you and/or your unborn fetus? Or, have you ever eaten coin-flavored cereal? Or, how about this, have you ever smelled yourself in the bathroom and nearly fainted, or tried to hold your own nose because you couldn't tolerate your own smell?

Well, you will probably experience any or all of these "issues" after you become pregnant. Maybe you won't experience the whole fatal-air-in-the-vagina thing. But you will worry about it. From experience I can tell you that having children is one of my life's greatest experiences. From that same experience, however, I can also tell you that pregnancy sucks @$$! There was never a time in my life (or in the lives of many of the women I consulted while writing this book) where I felt more out of control. Between my expanding girth, exhaustive

14

symptoms, and emotional fragility, I was a ticking time bomb, and for the first time in our lives, I think my husband was actually afraid of me. Like, seriously. I would go from crying during a commercial to screaming about someone leaving a cup of fruit punch on the countertop (the color red made me nauseous while I was pregnant). My husband thought he was in his own version of *The Exorcist*.

The simple truth is that, as a pregnant woman you are going to experience things you never thought possible. Some of those "experiences" might include simultaneous diarrhea and constipation, unruly inverted and/or hairy nipples, gas like a trucker, an appetite to rival any football team, torturous sleep deprivation, random anonymous pain, and dental damage. And that is only the tip of the iceberg! Some of those symptoms will be discussed in this funny little book. So put your feet up and enjoy!

# A – ADVANCED sense of smell

I smell stinky people…

Have you ever smelled someone's morning breath in the evening? Or had someone walk by you and you could smell that they forgot to use deodorant? Have you ever had a conversation with someone and at the end of it you could tell what they had for lunch? And you know it included onions, garlic, and sardines? Well, welcome to pregnancy. When you're pregnant you have the sense of smell of a trained canine. You can smell everything with vivid clarity: steak on the grill a mile away, gasoline without a gas station in sight, and grass on the ground. Unfortunately, that vivid sense of smell also extends to people who wear strong – and maybe cheap – perfume, who may not have worn deodorant, or who have bad breath.

I was once shopping for a new nightgown to wear in the hospital when I was to give birth to my first son. I was about 8 1/2 months pregnant. I had found a lovely yet comfortable nightgown and was proceeding to checkout but I could not get to the checkout line because of the foul odor coming from the lady behind the register. She was not funky, but her perfume nearly knocked me off my feet. I had to leave the gown there and return later with my hubby – just in case the offending lady was there.

While pregnant I could not stand the smell of toothpaste (which made brushing my teeth anything but fun), noodles (which before I was pregnant I didn't even know had a smell) and anything red. I couldn't stand the smell of pasta sauce, fruit punch, watermelon, apples. Literally, the color red had an offensive smell when I was pregnant. When you are pregnant, you can all but smell what someone is thinking. Loads of fun, right?

# B – BREASTS sagging

Down down baby
Down by the roller coaster
Sweet sweet baby
I'll never let you go…

As someone who is thinking of starting a family, have started a family, just likes kids, or whatever; I will bet that you have probably heard of the *Down Down Baby* childhood song. And maybe as you read it as this chapter's heading, it made you smile. Did it evoke images of little children playing? Or make you think of having a precious baby girl? Were you envisioning her in a pretty dress, with pretty ribbons in her hair, singing this song as she played with her little girlfriends, only pausing long enough from play to look at you with pride as you looked back at her adoringly?

Awww, what a sweet image! I'll bet what you DIDN'T think as you read the lines of this popular children's song, was that the *Down Down Baby* lyrics would be referring to your breasts.

Down down baby, down by the roller coaster... Yes, roller coaster is a good description of what pregnancy in general will feel like for a lot of women. There will be good days (where you manage to hold on to at least most of your breakfast) and there will be bad days (where you forget that breakfast didn't always taste like copper). Like the proverbial roller coaster, there will be plenty ups and downs with pregnancy. But, there will also be plenty ups and downs with your breasts.

If you were lucky (as some of us were) "perky" was probably a word you and maybe even others used to describe your breasts. You may remember how they stood at attention, and how you could go without wearing a bra. I consulted with many mommies while writing this book and one of them tells this true story: Anna[1] recalls a few years back having a man (and a woman) comment on how beautiful and high her breasts sat. She was wearing a spaghetti-strap cute little top that required she go bra-less, and her "girls" (also known as breasts, boobs, chicas) stood high and proud, ready to take on the day. The woman in question, being secure in her own femininity commented that Anna's breasts were "very perky and high."

In the woman in question's defense, Anna noted that she was a good friend and such a comment was okay to make. The guy in Anna's story commented that he wished they would fall out of her top so he could catch them. Anna didn't know that the guy had said that at the time. Anna and a group of friends were out having dinner for her then-boyfriend (now husband)'s birthday and her then-

---

[1] Not her real name. All names were changed to protect anonymity.

boyfriend told her after the fact. The conversation went something like this:

Then-boyfriend to Anna (while beaming proudly): "Oh, by the way, (blank) made a comment about your breasts. Apparently he couldn't keep his eyes off them."

Anna to then-boyfriend (while frowning with righteousness): "Oh, yeah? Well, what did he have to say?"

Then-boyfriend (while attempting to look like he was ashamed of his friend, but was really proud that his friend was checking Anna out): "Oh, he just said that he was watching them all night, hoping that one would fall out."

Anna (angrily): "What?!"

Then-boyfriend (realizing that he probably shouldn't have told Anna this): "Yeah, he said he would've gladly caught it for you."

Anna (gasping, not realizing she would one day long for her "perky" breasts to be the object of someone other than her husband's desires): "He's an idiot!"

Today that conversation might go a little bit differently. I imagine there would be a lot more "thank you's" and blushing on Anna's part. How many of us mommies can sympathize with Anna? Don't we wish someone would desire our "girls" again! Or, even better, refer to them as perky!

For many, the days of strapless tops and bountiful B/C cups are gone. They have been replaced with double D's that swing. And God forbid if you already had double D's! Those new and improved suckers are likely to require their own zip code and/or parking pass!

Michelle is another mommy who can relate. She shared with the group that her husband used to tell her that when she would exit out of a swimming pool the song "Brick House" by The Commodores would play in his head.

A "Brick House" woman refers to a woman with all the right curves. This woman might be beautifully proportioned (or "stacked") in her hips, her butt might be just right, or her breasts might sit high and perky. Michelle lamented to the group that the new song that comes to mind when she gets out of the pool, at least to herself, is the old spiritual hymn "Wade in the water, Wade in the water children, Wade". Yes, ladies, Anna and Michelle are like so many women who can recall having "girls" that once reached for the sky, but that are now reduced to skimming the surface of the water.

# C – CONSTIPATION

Root-beer flavored, chocolate laxative candy bars

Dara was embarrassed to say this. But, she decided to figuratively let it all hang out. According to Dara, be prepared to go as long as a week or more without pooping. With her first pregnancy, it took her two weeks to have a bowel movement. This extreme constipation occurred during her first trimester, right around the time she found out she was pregnant. Despite eating prunes, drinking prune juice, taking laxatives, ingesting castor oil, and eating what she described as some sort of horrific-tasting, root-beer flavored chocolate laxative candy bar, she simply could not go. Her body was too busy making a person to concern itself with eliminating waste. So she sat in discomfort for two weeks dragging around old feces. On top of that, she was pregnant and couldn't stop eating even though her body wasn't letting anything out. Can you say ouch?

# D – DIARRHEA

Diarrhea, anyone?

Oh, but when it does come, it comes. Dara went from constipated in her first trimester to home in bed with diarrhea during her third trimester.

Quite the opposite happened where she went from constipation to full-blown diarrhea because her body was stretched to capacity with a child, and it seemingly refused to take in any more food. Her body simply sent the food right back out while still in its original liquefied form.

On one day in particular, after a trip out to dinner with her husband, she playfully reflects on how their ride home from dinner turned into something out of a scene from *The Amazing Race* with the two of them in mad pursuit of a toilet. Between Dara and that glorious public toilet stood every obstacle imaginable, with the exception of leaps from tall buildings and solving difficult puzzles.

Maybe there were no leaps from buildings or actual puzzles to solve, but at one point Dara recalls that she did have to "figure out" how to run as fast as she could while still tightly constricting her butt muscles – i.e. "holding it in." She had to do both of those mutually exclusive things while also ignoring her husband who was laughing hysterically in the parking lot of the bank as she ran to save her dignity, and her cream-colored pants. Now *that* takes skill.

# E – EMOTIONAL

Piss off, a$$hole; and other terms of endearment

Get ready to become emotional. Yes, I know you've been warned that you might cry at the drop of a hat, and that certain unexplained events might reduce you to tears. For Stacy it was commercials.

Whether it was the loving way that a mom wiped up her family's mess with a Brawny double-textured paper towel, or the way the Pampers commercial showed snapshots of many beautiful babies, Stacy could cry easily - and often. But she expected that.

What she did not expect were the flashes of red-hot, hormonally-induced, psychotically-expressed anger. Like the time she was in the supermarket and was skipped in the line; Stacy shamefully reported that her instinct had been to rip the lady's throat out. Even as she told us this story, the harshness of such a thought made her openly flinch. But back then, while pregnant and emotionally unstable, Stacy begrudgingly admitted that she would have gladly dislocated that lady's collarbone, and gone home to eat warm cookies and milk. Oh yeah, and cry on the paper towel commercials.

Hell hath no fury like a hot, fat, hungry, pregnant woman standing in line with swollen feet. Just ask the Hulk, I mean Stacy (and do it nicely).

# F – FLINSTONE feet

Free shoes to a good home

Take one last adoring and lustful look at your size 7 red pumps. You know the ones. Then let's get ready to do a little bit of math.

$X = 1 + y + (z)$;

Where,

$X$ = size your feet will become

$y$ = your size now

$z$ = number of children you have or will have

Using my made-up, though surprisingly accurate formula, if you used to be a size 7 pre-pregnancy ($y=7$), then you have 1 child ($z = 1$) you can rest assured that those size 7 feet will become size 9's. Where, $X = 1 + (7) + (1) = 9$ ($X = 9$). If you have 2 children and were a size 7 to begin with you will likely become a size 10 ($1+7+2 = 10$). You can subtract .5 if you have beautiful shoes. This is because the sheer desperation to get back into them will make you tolerate wearing a shoe that's a half size too small. But that's the best I can do. You will get bigger. Your feet will stretch, and that includes the bones in your feet. And even when (or if) you lose the baby weight, the bones will still remain stretched out. There is no going back.

Think of a pair of stockings or socks. Once you've stretched them out, do they ever return to their original tightness? Go ahead, test the theory. Lay a pair of socks side by side, stretch one out and leave the other alone. Once you're done stretching one of the socks, doesn't it remain just a bit longer that the other sock? The same will be true for your feet.

Still, you don't have to get rid of your pretty shoes. You can stack them up really pretty and look at them from time to time like you would an inspirational poem. They are wonderfully therapeutic. And also, now that you can't fit the old shoes, you have a bona fide ~~excuse~~ reason to shop for new ones. Just don't do your final replacement shopping until you're done having children.

# G – GAS

Port-o-potties and you

Have you ever used a port-o-potty in the middle of Bourbon Street after Mardi Gras celebrations? Let Hannah paint a picture for you. Mardi Gras, or Fat Tuesday as it's known to some, is a day-long celebration that starts around 3 a.m. and ends at midnight. Actually, the festivities leading up to Mardi Gras start about two weeks prior to Mardi Gras day, and culminate at midnight on Fat Tuesday.

In any case, according to Hannah, Popeyes Chicken is the flavor of the day on Mardi Gras. Hannah proudly asserts that it is not unusual to have a line of customers wrapped around Popeyes and down the street on Mardi Gras day starting as early as 5 a.m. Yep. You heard right. Fried chicken and red beans for breakfast.

Well, if you haven't already heard, beans are very fibrous and are great at inducing and promoting regularity. Add the red beans, fried chicken and hot, buttery biscuits to the other foods served on Mardi Gras, such as hot dogs, hamburgers, hot sausage and shrimp po-boys and alcohol, and you have a surefire party – in your tummy.

Having set the menu, go with Hannah if you will as she sets the scene. Imagine groups of thousands of people filtering onto a normal-sized city street. These rowdy people have been out all night; they've been eating red beans and fried chicken for breakfast and drinking like fish. And they all have a handful of port-o-potties to share on one of the world's busiest and filthiest streets, on one of the world's most popular days. Not surprisingly, what goes in must come out.

The port-o-potties on Bourbon Street and in the French Quarter have an indescribable smell. Hannah unabashedly reports that if she had to give a clue as to what a port-o-potty might smell like, boiled dog poop laid out in the sun, and fresh animal corpses comes to mind. And that, according to Hannah, is probably putting it mildly.

So why, you wonder, is she talking about the smell of port-o-potties during a conversation among women about what should go in a book about "not-so-pretty" pregnancies. That is because Hannah asserts that while you are pregnant, the smells that come out of you will smell like the port-o-potties she just described. Hannah admits that her smell in the bathroom was like the smell of death warmed over. She insists that you too will wonder what you ate to make you smell like fried, sweaty testicles. Or how it is that your own smell makes you sick?

Hannah, in her ever-so-colorful way asked the group this question: "Have you ever used the bathroom while pregnant and couldn't stomach your own smell?" An overwhelming majority of the group raised their hands in agreement. Well, guess what, you too will more than likely know what that feels like. If you are having a baby then you will probably know very soon what that *smells* like. Just remember, Hannah tried to warn you.

# H – HUNGER

Hungry hungry hippo

Is it your fantasy, like it was mine and most of the women in the group, to eat what you want, when you want, how you want during pregnancy? Did you imagine that pregnancy would be a time to indulge your innermost childlike desires? Like eating ice cream for breakfast, and birthday cake for dinner? Or an entire cheesecake for a snack? Did you envision hanging out with your own custom-ordered box of donuts?

Well, what if you not only could eat all day long, but HAD to eat all day long? This happens in pregnancy. With Mary Ellen's first pregnancy she ate every 2 hours, like clockwork. With her second, in the first trimester, she had to eat every hour.

The thing they don't tell you is that sometimes your body hates the good, fun foods. Instead, your body craves protein, so you might have to eat things like peanut butter all day. Or your body might crave fruit, so you're reduced to days upon days of apples. Or your body might sometimes crave foreign and sometimes potentially dangerous substances, such as chalk, mud, dirt, or painted wall chips. For many of us, your body literally betrays you by rejecting the fun stuff like donuts, cake, and ice cream and craving the dull stuff like broccoli (unseasoned because the smell of spices makes you sick), or plain peanut butter.

During Mary Ellen's second pregnancy she recalls that she was starving all the time. She says she literally could not get full. And according to Mary Ellen it wasn't a fun "I think I'll have a nice, thick, juicy steak" sort of eating. It was the "if I don't eat something right this second I am going to peel over in pain" type. See, the thing they don't tell you is that hunger during pregnancy can be painful and extremely uncomfortable. Because your body is working hard around the clock it requires almost constant replenishment. And your system will feel like it is on the verge of shutting down (read: weakness and physical pain) if you don't feed it immediately.

In my case, during my second pregnancy, the smell and sight of sweets made me nauseous. But I had to have protein and I had to have it immediately. I am not a peanut butter fan, but I would pack jars of the stuff to take with me the way some people pack bottled water. I had a jar of peanut butter for middle of the night bathroom runs, I had a jar of peanut butter on my nightstand, and a jar of peanuts in my purse. Not a bag. A jar. Having eaten so much peanut butter during my pregnancy, to this day, the sight of peanuts makes me gag.

There is a difference between wanting to eat for fun and having to eat so you won't pass out. The latter you will experience. Think mandatory food eating contest. During pregnancy, you will be enrolled in that contest on a daily basis. Happy, gorging!

# I – INDIGESTION

## Indigestion and heartburn

Imagine, if you will, someone taking a Brillo pad to the inside of your chest and rubbing vigorously. Or lighting a raging fire just behind your chest wall. Sounds lovely, right? Indigestion and heartburn during pregnancy are bad enough to make you want to drown yourself, just to take in enough water to alleviate the burning in your chest.

When Erica was pregnant, she explains how she had so much heartburn and indigestion that she would try to sneak up on it. She would try to toss back ice cold water in an attempt to wash the fire away. She tried Tums. She even desperately tried deep breaths and sharp inhales to soothe the fire burning in her chest. Nothing worked.

An old wives tale is that heartburn is indicative of your baby having a lot of hair at birth. In Erica's (and mine, as well as nearly every woman in the group's) case it was true. Erica had deadly heartburn with her first pregnancy and her son was born with a head (and neck) full of hair. She had no heartburn (thank, GOD!) during her second pregnancy and observed that her son's head was nearly as bald as his butt. That aside, Sharon warns that the heartburn will be so bad that you might actually consider reaching down into the back of your throat and rubbing the area, or pulling the kid out and giving him or her a haircut. For her that's how bad it was. Oh, the joys of pregnancy.

# J – JINX

An Ode to Mother-in-laws

Hate your mother-in-law? Don't be too surprised when your child comes out looking like her. Thought that kid at the store was annoying? Add annoying to the list of your child's possible traits.

There is something telling about expectations and karma. When Isabelle's mom was pregnant with her, she did not like her mother-in-law and according to Isabelle's father her mom had said some things to that effect. Well, guess who Isabelle looks like? When Isabelle was pregnant with her daughter, her family would play this record about a fair-skinned, Italian child. Isabelle is Italian and is a beautiful, rich, olive-tone, and her husband is equal in complexion, if not a bit darker-skinned. Well, sure enough, Isabelle's daughter is so light-skinned that some family and friends jokingly say that she's clear.

The point is, watch what you say, watch who you're mean to, and what you "speak up" about while pregnant. You might find yourself face-to-face with that annoying neighbor, or not so attractive co-worker. Can you imagine them calling you "mommy"? Our children's souls are like banks, so watch what you deposit into them.

# K – KICKING

Many women think their baby's in-utero kicks are beautiful and they cannot wait until the day comes when they get to experience this amazing phenomenon. Whether for the first time in a first pregnancy or the 100th time during the 3rd pregnancy, it is still a beautiful thing. And I am one of those women who thinks so. But it is also freaky as hell.

What they don't tell you is that the experience can be a bit "extra-terrestrial". Sort of like a cross between the movie *Alien* and the TLC show *A Baby Story*. Just imagine if you were sitting at home on the sofa chowing down on a bowl of cereal (you'll probably eat lots of that because the folic acid is good for you and baby) and you notice an entire foot really slowly and menacingly-like creep across your abdomen. It is quite possibly one of the scariest things you will ever encounter outside of a strange man chasing you up a barren road with a chainsaw.

And at least then the horrific terror is not going on inside of you.

The first time I saw one of my sons' elbows jut across my stomach with enough force to make my blouse flutter, I nearly took off running. But where do you run to when the horror is in your belly? Just be prepared to scare yourself, and others, when your little ET makes contortionist-like appearances under your skin.

# L – LEAKS

You are in the height of your youth, or even if you're an older woman like Leigh, if you're thinking of having children I'm sure you thought you had a few more good years in you before Depends commercials would become appealing. But, lo and behold, being pregnant brings out the toddler in you because, in addition to possibly finding yourself in a situation where you'll have to squeeze your butt cheeks to stop yourself from boo-booing in your undies like Dara, you might have to use those good ole' kegels to stop yourself from wee-weeing on yourself.

When you're pregnant everything loosens up down below and you become more prone to wetting yourself. But that's not the only leak you are likely to spring. Can you say "leaky nipples?" Never thought those were words that would come out of your mouth, did you? Well, not only might your nipples leak milk, they will do so unexpectedly and oh-so-

47

noticeably. You will learn to do a quick look-see at your boobs the way some men have perfected the quick look-see for their zipper flys.

It will look like someone placed two watery drinks on opposite sides of your chest. Have you ever seen the round wet circles a glass leaves on the table when it perspires and doesn't have a coaster under it? That "look" will be repeated across your shirt on many occasions. And last I checked, there is not a way to inconspicuously tie a sweater across your boobs as you would have your waist while in Junior High School. But if you figure out how to do that, please let the rest of us know.

# M – METALLIC taste

## Eggs, toast, and a side of pennies

We all know about morning sickness, so I won't go into too much detail about that. What I will say is that when you finally can keep some food down, don't be surprised when it tastes like pennies. No, pennies are not the latest nouveau French dish. I actually mean pennies. Like .01 cent, copper coins.

When Felice was pregnant with her children, her first child especially, everything she ate tasted metallic, like she had run her tongue along the inside of someone's coin purse. To say it was annoying is an understatement. If you'd like to know what it feels like, Felice recommends you try this. Eat a meal, and after every bite of whatever you eat, lick a penny. Did it? Well, welcome to pregnancy!

# N – NAUSEA

Nausea is as synonymous with pregnancy as are pickles and late night runs to the store for ice cream. So what is it they don't tell you? They don't tell you what all will make you nauseous. For me, during the first trimester of my first pregnancy it included every food except red apples, ginger snaps, and frosted flakes sans milk. Then the list became a bit more sophisticated and items/things such as slushies, dog food, dogs, and any type of meat other than fish made me nauseous.

Oh, but my last trimester took the proverbial cake, and I became nauseated by the smell of the inside of my car. And keep in mind the seats were leather (not cloth), but apparently the smell of the inside of my beautiful, clean, convertible BMW 328ic was enough to make me park my car for my entire last trimester. Imagine how frustrating it was to have to use my hubby's dirty car with everything from gym socks on the floor to old coffee mugs in the cup holders because I could not tolerate the smell of my beautiful - and clean - car.  Oh, the injustice.

My second pregnancy became even more frustrating when I became nauseated by even the thought of all my favorite junk foods, and by the color red. Yes, the color red, in all its shapes, sizes, and textures sent me retching to the bathroom. Some of the offending red items included: red apples, pasta sauce, fruit punch, watermelon, and strawberry jam or jelly. And morning sickness? Somebody (probably a man) was playing a sick joke when they named it morning sickness, because for many women it occurs all day long. I know it did for me, as well as for several other women in the group.

Try being nauseated by the smell of outside (2nd pregnancy, 3rd trimester) all day long. It certainly makes the day that much more challenging when the smell of outside makes you sick. Who even knew that "outside" had a smell?

# O – OILY skin

Just plain ole slippery

"Oh, my, look at how you're glowing." Actually, that "glow" that others praise soon-to-be moms for, seasoned moms actually know as just plain old oiliness. Your face might resemble a pizza when you are pregnant because of all the greasiness. It might also resemble a pizza in texture because of the aforementioned greasiness.

When Christina was pregnant, she says that her face was so oily that the oil would literally pick up her makeup and carry it down her face. Think: mudslide. She jokingly told the group that she used to have to wipe her forehead so often with a cloth that onlookers probably thought she had just delivered her first sermon. She confided that she had always thought that she would have a beautiful "I-am-woman-who-gives-life" kind of glow that would make people run after her in the mall to find out her secret. She says the last thing she thought was that her skin would revert back to its reckless adolescent pubescent behavior.

But unlike as a pubescent adolescent, pregnant women cannot use the many skin creams out there to control their raging mudslide of a face. So, we're just stuck. Why, aren't you pretty?

# P – PEEING

Pee wee Herman takes on a new meaning

I hope I am not being crude when I say this, but, get ready to pull your pants down more than you did when you were trying to conceive. Honestly. You will pee all day and night. It's like the baby is sitting on your bladder and the second it fills up with even an ounce of fluid he or she presses the "release fluid now" button and off you go.

This constant peeing becomes even more annoying (1) as you grow fatter and fatter and simply want to be off your feet (and not on them headed to the toilet 15 times a day) and (2) because its takes you long enough to get to sleep anyway being as uncomfortable as you are (read: hot and fat) and trying to find a comfortable position to sleep in only to have to get out of it to pee for the 129th time in 2 hours.

But what takes the cake and makes peeing all night (and day) the worst situation ever is when you have gotten up to pee for the 129th time in 2 hours and you come back to bed only to find your hubby or partner nestled comfortably between the sheets, uninterruptedly sleeping the night away. In that case, you may do what some of us women in the group have done to even the scales and rectify this unjust and unlawful practice of nature. And that is, wake your hubby up every time you must go, and if you really want to torture him, start talking about your feelings or something. After all, you're both in this together (smiley face).

# Q – QUESTIONS about everything

Anxiety and the "What-If" game of life

Get ready to start worrying about everything. Can I eat sushi? How about tilapia? How harmful is coffee? Is my seatbelt too tight? Will my airbag hurt my baby if I am in a car accident? I didn't feel a kick, should I have? Can the baby smell that cigarette across the room? Should I perm/dye my hair? Will the baby be healthy? Can I afford this baby? Will I be able to give him/her everything they want and need?

And that is just the beginning. Those are the types of concerns you'll have before you even meet this baby. They quadruple after your precious bundle gets here. Get ready to become a mama bear. Should my toddler eat that? Should I breastfeed? For how long? What if I can't? Does that make me a bad mother? Am I a bad mother because I am leaving my baby to go back to work? What if they won't take great care of my baby? Will my baby know the caregiver more than it knows me? Am I setting my baby up to become needy since I am not there with him/her during their crucial months? What if my child gets kidnapped or abused? What if they get bullied?

Let's also discuss some of dad's worries, because even the most carefree dads might change their tunes after baby comes. Dad's worries: What if I lose my job and can't support my family?  What if our lives change and become all about the baby? Will I still get sex after baby comes? Will I still feel the same about my partner's vagina after seeing a person come out of it?

Oh, the fun you two will have on a Friday night!

# R – ROUND ligament pain

Seizures and such

I've got three words for you: Round Ligament Pain. Sounds innocent enough, right? Well listen to this, and please remember that I am an intelligent woman. Because it is entirely possible that you might forget that while reading this.

Honest story: while brushing my teeth one morning – which itself was no small feat since toothpaste made me nauseous – I got a tremendous pain near the bottom of my stomach. I was about 8 months pregnant and home alone. The pain took hold of the lower half of my body and squeezed. I held on to the sink for dear life and just allowed my body to do what it wanted to do, which at that moment was constrict. When that pain let me go I was floored. I had never felt anything like that before in my life. I looked up and saw my refection in the bathroom mirror. I was foaming at the mouth! Then I knew! I knew why I had had the pain I'd had. I was having a seizure! I ran out of the bathroom and down the hall screaming for my mom, my husband, and Jesus – in no particular order. Since no one was there, I knew I had to save my own life and the life of my unborn child. I called my Ob-Gyn[2], pressed the number indicating it was an emergency and was connected right away to a nurse. She got on the line and I frantically explained that I was having a seizure, complete with body convulsions and foaming at the mouth. Fast-forward about 30 life-altering seconds and the nurse concluded that I was having round ligament pain at worst, Braxton Hicks at best, and the "foaming at the mouth" was actually just leftover toothpaste. (Remember I had been brushing my teeth? Well, apparently, I'd forgotten). Needless to say, I was so embarrassed at my next doctor's appointment and neither my Ob-Gyn (nor my husband and family) would let me live that down.

---

[2] Obstetrician/Gynecologist

Before you right me off as the stupidest person alive, look at the keyword in round ligament pain. That word is pain. The pain was so bad that the only thing I could imagine was that it was a seizure. So don't believe the hype when they tell you that it's only a little bit of discomfort. If it was discomfort, then it would be called round ligament discomfort. It's called round ligament *pain*. And that pain was bad enough to send me running out the bathroom, toothpaste "foaming" at the mouth, believing I'd had a seizure. So as much as that will tell some of you that I am a little bit "off," I hope it tells you that it was just that painful.

# S – S-T-R-E-T-C-H marks

S-t-r-e-t-c-h marks everywhere

Elizabeth, our resident diva, divulged that she had once had an idea to throw a 70's inspired Halloween party simply because she'd found a brown and gold tiger-striped (or some kind of animal-striped) cat suit. Back then she was a "Brick House" and was looking for any excuse to fit all of her "sexiness" into that tiger-striped cat suit.

Well, the party never happened, because for one, she spent all of her "party years" in school pursuing a higher education, which didn't leave a lot of time for parties. But who would've thought she'd get a second chance to rock a tiger-striped cat suit?

Elizabeth said she never expected she'd get that chance, and she certainly never expected that the tiger-striped cat suit would become a permanent bodysuit. Thanks to the wonderful world of stretch marks Elizabeth gets to wear that once fantasized

61

about tiger-striped cat suit every time she goes anywhere. She wears it under her clothes. She wears it in the shower. She wears it as her birthday suit. Thanks to her beautiful children, Elizabeth has flesh-colored stretch marks everywhere, against what used to be flesh-colored skin. And, guess what ladies? As Elizabeth reports, and as most us already knew, the creams, oils, serums, and gels do not work.

Have you ever noticed how they take an actress or supermodel and lather them and their tummies down with makeup and then exclaim to us, "Look, this supermodel woman didn't get stretch marks because she used (fill in the blank)!" Trust us ladies, it doesn't work.

Stretch marks are a result of the elasticity of the skin stretching and tearing. No cream or oil is going to realign those tears and put them seamlessly back together. At best, one or two of these creams/oils/serums might fade the stretch marks to where they are less noticeable and maybe not jumping off your skin, with a sign that says, "Look at me! Look at me!"

It's a sad truth ladies, but the best we can do is try to diminish our stretch mark scars, or we can choose to sport them like they are our own custom-made tiger-striped cat suits. You go, grrrl!

# T – TIREDNESS

Sleep? What's that?

To do: complete a triathlon, build an oceanfront property, travel across Montana herding buffalo, sweep the streets of New York, and cook dinner for Oklahoma. Even if that is not your to-do list, then that is what you will feel like you've just done when you're pregnant. And you'll feel like you've done those things for about three months straight.

There is no tiredness like the tiredness felt by a pregnant woman, especially one in her first trimester. And if you're one of the lucky majority, that tiredness – perhaps to a minimally lesser extent – will return in the third trimester. So let's do the math. If a woman spends 3 months of the first trimester and 3 months of the third trimester exhausted, then that's roughly half a year that she feels like she is competing in an Iron Man competition. And that doesn't include the resurgence of tiredness she will feel once baby gets home and wants to eat on every commercial, or every time a Law *and Order* episode airs, which is approximately every 8 minutes.

Basically, to make it easier on yourself, from the time you find out you're pregnant, just go ahead and count on being exhausted for the rest of your life. Oh, except for about a 6-12 week period during the second trimester when the baby gives you enough energy to catch your breath before he or she finishes you off. If you think I am exaggerating, ask any pregnant woman anywhere at any time. And if that pregnant woman says she is not tired, bet her $4.59 that she is in her second trimester and you'll win every time. And if you'd like to do a follow up study, ask the parents of young children if they are STILL tired, and listen for the resounding "YES!" that you will hear, or "HELL, YES!" (depending on how close to a church you are). I don't think you'll rest again until your children go off to college, and you probably won't rest then either because you'll be too worried that they're out drinking and partying or wasting your hard-earned, tuition payment money.

Leslie tells a story she heard about a couple who used to fix their children's cereal and put it outside of their bedroom door on Saturday mornings with instructions for the children to turn on the T.V. to whatever cartoon they wanted to watch. That way, when the children awoke and bounded down the hallway to their parents' room they would get their breakfast and a cartoon, and mom and dad would get a little extra sleep. Leslie confided that before she had children she had thought that that was the most neglectful thing she'd ever heard. After she had children, however, she considered starting a fan club for the couple who thought of that genius idea.

PS. Sleep deprivation is an effective method of torture. Need I say anymore?

# U – UGLY BETTY

Ugly Betty

I have 10 words for you. Acne, thinning hair, rolls of fat, and a swollen nose. No, that is not the title of a bad country song. It is the reality that many women experience during pregnancy.

Picture this scene: A pregnant supermodel-esque woman steps out of her car. It just so happens to be a two-seater sports car with batman doors, despite the fact that she is pregnant. We guess she'll figure out the whole car seat situation later. Her hair is blowing despite the fact that there is no wind. Apparently she carries around her own turbo fan. She is pregnant as you can barely see from her cute-as-a-button little pregnancy bump protruding ever so gently out of her all-too-cute designer top. She is in skinny jeans with 6 inch heels, despite the fact that she is pregnant. There are no issues with equilibrium or balance as she perches ever so perfectly on her stiletto needle-point heels. Her skin is flawless with the prettiest glow. It's as if a flashlight is being shone on her cheeks. Is a flashlight being shone on her cheeks? You look around for the flashlight. Ok, there is none, so you go back to your silent admiration of her. Her hair stops blowing from her invisible fan just long enough for you to see that it sleekly falls just above her butt. She walks by you and shines the most brilliant smile, and wouldn't you know it, she smells like heaven.

Ok. Believe that commercial for "getting a great haircut, or buying a new two-seater, or owning an invisible fan" if you want to, but that is not the reality of pregnancy for most women. As it concerns you and this group of women, expect this scene: You stumble out of your SUV as a container of french fries from McDonald's stumbles out behind you. Apparently you lost your footing because you're pregnant and the pressure on your uterus is throwing your equilibrium off. The pack of french fries fell out of your cup holder where you had so precariously perched them so you could quickly get to them to eat. Again. You are in a 5-seater because you have a little one on the way, and maybe even another not so little one already here. Your hair is not blowing, because it is pinned up. And it is pinned up because if you don't pin it up it might fall right out of your head. Or if you are lucky enough to be like some of the pregnant women whose hair grows in long and full, then it's tangled and unkempt because you didn't comb it. And you didn't comb it because you were tired from tossing and turning all night as you lugged that huge belly from left to right.

Unlike the supermodel-esque pregnant woman in the commercial, it is obvious that you are pregnant because you are huge. And not in an *it-is-obvious-that-she-is-pregnant* kind of way. You are huge in an *I-wonder-if-she-is-pregnant-or-just-really-fat* kind of way. You are wearing flats because your feet are swollen and fat and, quite honestly, you wouldn't wear heels right now if it meant saving the world. Your skin resembles that of a 14 year old girl's, as it is full of acne. You have a pregnancy mask, making your neck appear three shades darker than your face, and making your face appear four shades darker than your body. Or if you're lighter-skinned, your pregnancy mask makes you look like you have Rosacea. Or like Santa Claus. And you probably don't smell so hot because the smell of deodorant, toothpaste and most lotions and perfumes make you nauseous.

We won't call you ugly. We'll just say you're attractively-challenged or the inverse of beautiful. Maybe you'll get lucky and this won't be you (yeah, right). But most likely it will. So just be prepared.

# V – VEINS

Pregnancy roadmap

For many, all of a sudden during pregnancy their body becomes a roadmap. There are veins across their legs, hands, arms, and big thick blue veins across their breasts. The blue veins were so thick and prominent across Teresa's breasts during her second pregnancy that anytime she wore a top that revealed any sort of cleavage her preschooler would say, "Mommy! Look! There's crayon on your chest!" She recalls that her preschooler probably thought daddy (her husband) had been drawing on mommy (Teresa).

What they tell you is that you will grow a "rack" that will rival any expensive boob job. What they don't tell you is that that "rack" might be streaked with blue veins that make you look like a long lost member of the Blue Man Group. The unsightly blue veins might make you want to cover those puppies up. And what's the point of having new and improved beautiful bountiful breasts if you're going to have to keep them hidden?

Additionally, other unattractive veins might pop up on your legs, your belly, and a few places in between. For many, pregnancy also marks an induction into the land of varicose veins, which can be an unattractive AND painful condition.

So let's get this straight: While pregnant, many if not most women will get bright unsightly veins on their breasts, tummy, and arms and legs. I guess that's not so bad if you live in Alaska or Antarctica and plan to go snow parka chic during your pregnancy. Oh, the joys of pregnancy.

# W – WEIGHT

Weight gain

Of course you know you will gain weight. But what they don't tell you is that the weight you gain may not be proportional to how much you eat.

Take Mya and Rachel as examples. Mya gained 51 pounds with her first son, but she couldn't stomach junk food. Whereas Rachel gained 28 pounds on a diet of ice cream and cookies. Mya's son was 7lbs 12.5 oz and Rachel's was 7 lbs 12 oz.

Also, the 51 pounds Mya gained caused so much pressure on her tailbone that it dislocated. Mya remembers that there was so much pain that when she sat or moved around it became unbearable. To try to ease the pain her OB[3]

---

[3] Obstetrician

recommended she carry around an inflatable seat cushion. She did, but says that it still hurt like hell.

Another thing they don't tell you is that there is no formula for how much you should gain. It's all up to your baby. Try telling a pregnant woman that she should only gain two pounds during the first couple months. You'd better duck, or at least brace yourself. A pregnant woman is eating because her body depends on it. She is eating because her body is using extra resources to build another person.

Like my grandmother says, "It boils my britches" when a male doctor (or female) explains to me or another woman that she should've only gained a certain amount of weight over a certain period. How do they know? Did they get an expense report from your body letting them know how much energy you expended and how much you need?

And if one more book tells one more pregnant woman they only need 300 extra calories a day to build a person, I'm going to scream. Who decided that it only takes the equivalent of two large apples or a couple tablespoons of peanut butter to build a person? That's like someone telling a contractor you only need a piece of tape and a thumb tack to build a house.

They tell us, "Don't eat like you're eating for 2 because one of you is really small." I say, don't eat for 2, eat for millions. Eat for the millions of cells you are producing as you grow a new life, the hundreds of bones you are developing. Eat when your body tells you you're hungry and stop when your body tells you you've had enough. That's the only way.

There are many women out there, including in our group, who are super interested in keeping their figures. Who isn't? But don't let the quest to maintain your figure make you give birth to a miniature baby. Eat like a life depends on it, because a life does.

# X – XTRA hair everywhere

Things G[4] never thought she'd do in a lifetime:

> Stand in the shower and very seriously contemplate how to shave the inside of her butt, because yes, there is hair there. And, according to her, there's lots of it.

> Sit on the lid of the toilet and shave her toes. Because yes, there is hair there also. And lots of it.

You too will be surprised where you grow hair. We have all heard horror stories of hair growing on nipples (as if there's not enough going on with those suckers), hair on knuckles, long hair in the nose, hair on upper lips (yes, some women grow mustaches capable of rivaling their husband's or

---

[4] Definitely not her real name. "G" had a really hard time sharing the fact that she had "butt hair" and wanted to make sure that her pseudonym was as bland as possible. So we only gave her an alphabet. Thanks for sharing, G!

partner's), hair in the ears, hair on the chin, hair on the small of the back, and extra thick hair on the va-jay-jay.

Ironically, for many women, including a few in our group, the hair on their heads begin to weaken, thin, or even fall out. And for those whose hair grows in long and lustrous, it falls out fast and furiously when baby makes his/her exit. As many mommies know, they might not catch you on one side, but they'll get you on the other.

# Y – YELLOW teeth

Yellow teeth and other dental damage

In addition to your hair, your skin, your breasts, your stomach, your uterus, your vagina, your thighs, and your feet, your teeth and gums will also take a beating.

What they don't tell you is that you become more susceptible to dental diseases such as Gingivitis and Periodontitis when you are pregnant. With these conditions, a pregnant woman is more likely to experience preterm labor and birth. As such, oral health is tremendously important during pregnancy!

As if that's not enough, toothpaste makes many women nauseous during pregnancy. Furthermore, if you're unable to brush normally, this might make your teeth begin to resemble a yellow highlighter. Since traditional toothpaste might make you nauseous (and if you're going to throw up, that defeats the purpose of brushing), you might be forced to try some sort of organic, tasteless, smell-less, effective-less, pseudo-toothpaste that tastes like dried children's glue. Moreover, at least a few of us are convinced that this abnormally-expensive concoction is nothing more than flour and water mixed together. It doesn't work, doesn't lather, doesn't taste good, and certainly doesn't clean our teeth. But at least it doesn't make us hurl.

In addition to being convinced that this flour-and-water concoction is a joke, we are convinced that the makers (i.e. mixers) of this ridiculous product are standing nearby the aisle where we might find this "toothpaste" laughing and high-fiving each other every time some hapless pregnant woman buys one of these. They can't believe their luck that we are so stupid to buy flour and water as toothpaste, and we can't believe our luck that we've found toothpaste that doesn't have a taste (and doesn't make us vomit). Now if we could only take our newfound luck and find Bigfoot or the Tooth Fairy, we could rack up!

# Z – ZOOM

Zoom = Loss of body shape

The zoom you see stands for your figure heading out the door. Don't believe the hype – or those who've been nip-tucked. Your body will NEVER be the same. Breasts will droop, or disappear forevermore. Muscle tone will be lost. Feet will grow. But it's only fitting because your entire life will change. Gone are the days of a Saturday afternoon in the mall shopping for the sexiest heels you can find for your date night with hubby. The new Saturday afternoon will be spent trying to doze as your little one sleeps, or trying to grab a shower, or maybe getting around to brushing your teeth. That date night will be replaced – if you find a babysitter – with a longing for extended sleep.

Ask the mommies in this group, or any mommy anywhere which they'd prefer, and the honest truth is that 9 out of 10 of us would prefer a nap over a night of movies, music, food, or sex. For new parents, a nap is the new dinner-and-a-movie. But back to your body. Kim said it best. She is a personal trainer who only gained 15 pounds while pregnant, and who took spinning classes up until her 7th month of pregnancy. She had her beautiful baby and dropped all the weight, but she readily admits that her body doesn't look the same. Her body fat composition rearranged and the body she had pre-pregnancy is not the body she has now. Even though she is still extremely fit, she admits that despite being a personal trainer for 7 years, no amount of crunches or abdominal exercises has gotten rid of the slight tummy bulge that she now has.

Now, of course there will be one woman out of 15 zillion who will swear that she got her body back and that she is the same as she was before, maybe even better. Do not believe this woman. She is trying to trick you. Or she is mistaken and misremembering the facts. Like Nancy who argued that she had gotten her body back within the first 6 weeks, but later admitted that she'd had a tummy tuck.

And for crying out loud, please do not believe these celebrities who swear they simply breastfed and everything popped right back into shape (like one Victoria's Secret supermodel said), or other celebrities who swear by the old "diet and exercise" spiel. Please rest assured that their "diet and exercise" regimen includes daily sessions with a personal trainer while the nanny watches their little one and the private chef whips them up a fat-free, gluten-free, cholesterol-free, calorie-free meal extravaganza.

Oh, and please don't believe Jennifer Hudson. None of us do.

For one, if you were already obese and then you start to do anything you are very likely to improve your body. But if you were obese and then start to work out with a personal trainer 5-6 days a week, and get paid millions of dollars to eat right, and you have the money to hire someone to make your meals for you (instead of grabbing what you can between bottle-feedings and diaper changes) and you have a nanny so that you can actually eat your specially prepared meals (instead of trying to scoff it down with your left hand while holding your baby with your right hand and his bottle with your chin), then of course you can not only get your body back but a better looking body than what you started with.

But I hate to have to tell you that you are not Jennifer Hudson and you are not a supermodel who is used to eating a cracker and a grape for dinner. You are Mrs. America, with things to do and children to raise, as well as dinner to cook, so don't expect to wake up and see your previous four-pack poking through your nightgown. What you'll see poking through your nightgown will be a symbol of your new identity and likely a little bit of flab left over from your sweet – though demanding – bundle of joy's short stay within you. Think of it as his parting gift to you.

## About TTP Publishing

*"Providing short and sweet books you can enjoy, when you're ready to enjoy them, that WON'T take all day...*

**...BECAUSE YOU HAVE THINGS TO DO."**

TTP Publishing is a book and media publishing company that specializes in publishing short books. It was founded by an avid reader who, after becoming a mom, doctor, bill-payer, and errand-runner, realized she had little to no time left in a day to sit back and enjoy a good book.

What's more, this busy mom was also impatient, meaning she not only wanted to sit back and enjoy a good book with her limited "me" time, but she also wanted to reach the conclusion of that book - without having to wait days or even weeks before she had more time to read again.

This busy mom had an "aha" moment as she thought of how awesome it would be if good books were shorter and lasted the length of say, a good movie, or dinner out.

That's when **TTP Publishing** - "TTP" stands for **to the point** - was founded.

TTP's books are sometimes funny, sometimes controversial, sometimes spicy, and sometimes tell-it-like-it-is, but they are almost always short and to the point...*because you have things to do.*

For information on submitting your book for publication, please visit us at www.ttppublishing.com, or send us an email to info@ttppublishing.com.

Happy Reading!!!

## TTP Publishing Books

*Act Like a CEO, Think Like a Millionaire: Why You Should Care LESS About What a Man or Woman Thinks About Love, Relationships, Intimacy and Commitment and MORE About GETTING WHAT YOU WANT OUT OF LIFE*

*What You WON'T Expect When You're Expecting Because This is The CRAP They Don't Tell You: ABC's of a Sucky Pregnancy*

*Confessions of a Surrogate for Celebrities*

*TESTIMONY: 10 Stories Detailing Supernatural Miracles, Blessings, and THE POWER OF PRAYER*

*Open Marriage: An Erotic Trilogy* (Book 1)

*Open Marriage: A.S.E. Sports Agency* (Book 2)

*Open Marriage: Behind the Scenes* (Book 3)

www.ingramcontent.com/pod-product-compliance
Lightning Source LLC
Chambersburg PA
CBHW071831020426
42331CB00007B/1688

* 9 7 8 0 9 8 5 5 9 8 8 9 1 *